GOLD

LADONNA J HITE

CLARITY INK, a FAITHTOGO company.

PO BOX 17273

SAN ANTONIO, TX 78217

DEDICATION

I left poverty for **LOVE**... Love in my heart!

ACKNOWLEDGMENTS

Everyone should **always** do good!

GOLD

"EXPLORE SUCCESS!"

"A MAN ASKED FOR MUCH...
BUT NOT **LOVE**!

LOVE IS MORE VALUABLE
THAN RUBIES!

LOVE IS THE KEY!"

"I FOUND OUT WHAT GOD REQUIRED OF ME! LOVE... INDUCED SUCCESS!"

"DON'T RISK YOUR THOUGHTS!"

"BETWEEN MY LEGS ARE JOY FOR A HEAD LEADER IN GODLY SUCCESS!

A MAN WHO WANTS TO DO RIGHT!

BE FAITHFUL FOR DUTY!

OUR DUTY IN LIFE... LOVE REQUIRES ME!"

"I REFUSE TO SHARE MY BED WITH AN UNFAITHFUL MAN!

WHAT'S FOR ME... IS MINE!

I GET TO KEEP ALL BY MYSELF!

INTIMACY, YUM YUM!"

"HUSBAND BE GLAD!

I AM A FAITHFUL WIFE!

YOU DIDN'T ASK GOD FOR A CHEATER! A CHEATING WIFE!"

“WHO KNOWS YOUR LEGS, YOUR THIGHS, YOUR HIPS... IN HOLY MATRIMONY?”

"GOD ORDAINS GOOD AND LOVELY STUFF FOR YOU TO ENJOY FOR THE REST OF YOUR LIFE!"

"TEACH YOUR CHILDREN HOW TO LOVE THEIR SPOUSE!

EACH ONE IS UNIQUE! LOVE THE DIFFERENCES OF EACH PERSONALITY OF AN INDIVIDUAL!

YOU CAN'T MAKE ALL MEN FIT ONE PERSONALITY, ONE INCOME, ONE OUTCOME!"

"GOD CREATED US ALL EQUAL IN THE BEGINNING!

SIN IS WHAT SEPARATED US!

EVOLUTION!"

"GOD WANTS MAN TO BE HONEST!

DON'T BE EMBARRASSING! EMBARRASSING HER! CHEATING! RULING HER UNFAIRLY!

WOMEN NEED LOVE... AND SO DO MEN! ALL MEN!

CHASTISEMENT HURTS DISOBEDIENCE! WHO'S WRONG? WHO'S RIGHT? LET GOD JUDGE BETWEEN THE TWO: HUSBAND AND WIFE HE SEES ALL HIDDEN SECRETS!"

"I FOUND OUT HOW STRONG **LOVE** IS!"

"I AM WILLING TO GET DRESSED FOR THE HONEYMOON!

HOW LOVELY!"

"'YOU ARE PRETTY IN YOUR POSTURE... YOUR FREAKY POSTURE! THAT SEXY POSE!' SAID THE HUSBAND TO HIS WIFE ON THEIR HONEYMOON NIGHT!

THE DAYLIGHT TOLD A SECRET!"

"DON'T DREAD SUCCESS... THE LOVE MAKING PROCESS!"

"LOVE IS INTIMATE! LUST IMITATES!"

"I'M NOT!

I'M NEVER GOING TO
IMITATE YOUR PAST
LOVERS!

LOOK AT MY NAME!"

"MAN IS EMPTY!

GOD IS FILLED UP WITH SUCCESS FOR A MAN OR WOMAN WHO HUNGER AND THIRST AFTER RIGHTEOUSNESS!"

"THE TRUTH HURTS! YET, THE PAIN IS BEARABLE... FOR HEALING!"

"I SIT HERE CONTEMPLATING LOVE THOUGHTS! AND THEY ARE DECENT IN STRUCTURE FOR LOVELY ROMANCE!"

"A MAN MAY TOUCH ME
BECAUSE THAT IS WHAT I
DESIRE!

MAY HIS LIPS STAIN
EVERY PART OF MY SKIN
WHERE LOVE, HIS LOVE IS
ENCOUNTERED! THAT IT
BRINGS ME
SATISFACTION AND JOY!
A TRAIL OF LUXURY IN
LOVE! THE LOVE MAKING
PROCESS!

OH HOLY MATRIMONY!

COMFORTABLE!

RELAX!"

"I AM EVIDENCE... LOVE! WHAT A GENTLE STROKE, SEEMINGLY!"

"SELL IT!

WHAT?

JOKE!

WHAT JOKE?

THE PUSSY DOES NOT LAUGH... IT SCREAMS IN THE JOYS OF EXCITEMENT!"

"THE PUSSY IS SERIOUS BUSINESS! MAKE IT MAD AND IGNORE IT! IT WILL BITE BACK IN STROKES AND THRUSTS OF THE HIPS!

THE PUSSY CONTROLS THE WHOLE BODY IN INTIMACY! GOOD LOVIN' INTIMACY!

PAUSE. BREAK. LET'S DO IT AGAIN!

ANGRY WET PUSSY!
LET THE MOUTH TELL IT!
CRYING!"

"SQUEEZE... PANT... INHALE... SUCK IN... PANT... I'M IN DEEP!"

"THE JOYS! INCREASE THE ERRATIC STRUCTURE OF THE CLIMB TO THE PEAK OF AN ORGASM!"

“MY ORGASM!
WHERE WILL IT FIND ME?

IN BED? ON A COUCH?
ON THE FLOOR?
IN A BATH?
IN THE SHOWER?
IN HIS ARMS?
IN A CAR?
IN A TRUCK, OR OTHER
MODE OF
TRANSPORTATION?
ON A COUNTERTOP,
TABLETOP... SOMETHING
STURDY TO HOLD OUR
BODIES TO FLOAT ON?”

"MAY LOVE TAKE ME EVERYWHERE!"

"LUST HAS SHOWN ME A
FOOL'S GOLD!
TEMPORARY SUCCESS IN
FOLLY!"

"MAY **LOVE** BE MY HERO FOREVER!"

"GOD IS LOVE!

JESUS IS LOVE!

MAY GOD AND HIS PRECIOUS SON JESUS SEND ME **LOVE**! THE ENCOUNTER OF A HUSBAND! ON A DISTINCT MARRIAGE MADE IN HEAVEN!"

"A CAMP!

MAY THE PURITY OF LOVE EXIST!

WHAT IS THE PURITY OF LOVE?

WHAT GOD SAYS IN THE HOLY BIBLE! THERE IS NO ARGUING ABOUT IT!"

"LUST WANTS TO VALIDATE AND ROAST EVERYTHING IT CAN FATHOM! AND YET, **LOVE** WILL STAND STRONG AS A SUPERHERO! AGAINST ITS FOE! A SPIRIT!"

"TODAY I WRITE... AND
LOVE IS MY DUTY!

LET ME DRENCH IN THE
SWEAT OF ROMANCING!
HOT OR COLD! I DON'T
WANT TO BE WARM IN MY
LOVE MAKING PROCESS!"

"I NEED PURPOSE!

YOU CAN FIGHT AND YELL
AT ME... I WILL STILL
WIN! **LOVE** WILL WIN
EACH STORM! YOU WILL
NOT WIN LUST! SEE ME?

I AM A CHAMPION!

MY NAME IS **L O V E**!
IT HAS MEANING!"

"I FOUND A BLESSING IN **LOVE**!

TO EACH ITS OWN!

I OWN THINGS FULL OF LOVELY SUPPORT!

'LOVE NEVER FAILS' SING IT!"

“THE MEDICINE...
BOOKS!”

"WHEN A MAN WANTS YOU TEMPORARILY, HE LACKS UNDERSTANDING! A WOMAN IS A TREASURE! HE DISHONORS HIMSELF!

A MAN WHO CHEATS ON HIMSELF BY DISHONORING HIS WIFE IS A FOOL!

HE LIED TO HIMSELF, 'I CAN GET AWAY WITH SIN!'"

"DON'T RUB UP ON SIN! ITS WOUND IS OPENED! DON'T CATCH IT! LUST IS POISONED SUCCESS! IT DOES HARM... GREAT HARM TO ITS USERS AND MAKERS OF ITS DEADLY SUBSTANCE!"

"I'M NOT ARGUING WITH A LIAR! WALK AWAY! WHO CAN STRAIGHTEN OUT MY LIFE? GOD CAN!"

"WHEN I AM OLD, I WANT TO BE REMEMBERED FOR... **LOVE**!"

LJ HITE

STRUGGLE MONEY

"YOU ARE A FRIEND!"

"DEBT WAS HERE BEFORE I WAS BORN... I WAS BORN IN DEBT! AN ECONOMY!"

"MY WHOLE LIFE IS TO WORK THE MONEY! TO PAY OFF WHAT BELONG TO ME! I HAD TO PAY FOR AN EDUCATION THAT OFFERED NO REFUNDS IF IT DIDN'T GRANT ME A PARDON OUT OF DEBT!"

"HOW CAN I GET OUT OF DEBT FAST?
EAT DEBT! SERIOUSLY! WE HAVE TO DEVOUR DEBT UNTIL IT DISAPPEARS OUT OF OUR LIVES! ONE BILL AT A TIME!"

"WHEN I WAS BORN I DIDN'T HAVE A BILL, SO THEY GAVE IT TO MY MOTHER INSTEAD! I WAS HER RESPONSIBILITY! HER OBLIGATION! BUT, WHERE DID MY FATHER RUN OFF TO? SKIPPING HIS WHOLE FINANCIAL OBLIGATION! BEING PARTIALLY RESPONSIBLE FOR MY CERTIFICATE OF A LIVE BIRTH!"

"WHY MUST MY MOTHER BEAR THE BURDEN OF THE LUXURY OF CHILDREN WHILE THE FATHER SKIPS HIS LIFE AWAY IN DECEIT?"

"WOMEN!

WOMEN WE ARE ALL HEALTHY!

LIFE DEMANDS JUSTICE!

WOMEN GIVE BIRTH TO MEN'S CHILDREN, WHILE MEN RUN AWAY!"

"I HAVE A BILL!
CHILD SUPPORT IS NOT
ENOUGH TO COVER IT!"

"A CHILD NEEDS A FATHER! THANK GOD FOR... GOD! HE IS THE GREATEST FATHER OF ALL TIMES!"

"YOU WICKED MEN...
DON'T JUDGE A WOMAN!
YOU CAME FROM HER!
A WOMB!"

“MAN WANTS TO TAKE EXISTENCE FOR HIS EXISTENCE! YET, HE COULD NOT DELIVER HIMSELF FROM A WOMAN'S SECRET PLACE... A PULSE!”

"DON'T DISRESPECT WOMEN... SELF!"

"EXCHANGE LOVE... GRANT GRACE!"

"A WOMAN CAN GIVE
BIRTH!
A BODY IS POWERFUL...
THOUGH, IN PAIN!"

"WICKED MOTHERS ARE A SHAME... AND SO ARE WICKED FATHERS!"

"WHEN A CHILD BURIES A WICKED MOTHER, IT IS A RELIEF! WHEN A CHILD BURIES A WICKED FATHER, IT IS A RELIEF! THE PAIN SUBSIDES! THE HORROR IS GONE!"

"PARENTS DON'T MISTREAT YOUR CHILDREN... CHASTISE THEM! CORRECT THEM! CORRECT THEIR WAYS INTO GOOD QUALITY THINGS! GODLY THINGS! HOLY THINGS!"

"THE BIBLE IS RIGHT! PROPHECY!"

"DON'T CONTINUE A GENERATION OF PAIN! GET AWAY FROM HORRIBLE DECEIT! PAIN! FREEDOM IS ALIVE! FREEDOM IS FREE! BREAK IT! THE CHAINS OF POVERTY! POVERTY OF THE SOUL!"

A LACK IN WISDOM

"I LEARNED HOW TO DO WELL!"

"GOD DID NOT BRING ME TO AFRICA TO DIE! THAT IS WHERE HISTORY AND LIFE BEGAN! HOW CAN THE GARDEN OF EDEN EXIST?"

"THERE IS NOTHING POOR IN AFRICA, BUT A MINDSET!"

“OCCUPATION! ESCAPE POVERTY IN YOUR MIND FIRST!”

GOLD

"YOU ARE A BALLOON SUCCESS!"

"HEALING POWER
BELONGS TO GOD! NO ONE
IS GREATER THAN GOD!
HE SENT US EVIDENCE OF
HIS LOVE FOR MANKIND!
A JEWISH MAN!
MAY I INTRODUCE HIM
PLEASE?
JESUS, THE CHRIST!

LET'S READ ABOUT HIS
HISTORY IN OUR HISTORY
BOOKS! OUR JEWISH
HISTORY BOOKS... THE
BIBLE! YOU TRANSLATE
IT FOR ME!"

"THE DEPTHS OF MY SOUL TRUSTS GOD! CAN YOU HEAR HIM? JESUS! HIS SON IS CALLING YOUR NAME?"

LJ HITE

SECRET

"SUPER!"

"NO ONE LOVES ME LIKE MY FATHER (GOD)! THAT IS A BORDER YOU CANNOT CROSS!

NO HUSBAND CAN MAKE ME UNDO MY LOVE I HAVE FOR THE FATHER, OUR HEAVENLY FATHER!"

TEARS

"MY TEARS CANNOT HIDE!"

"TEARS CANNOT WHISPER... THEY ARE A SIGN!"

"CAN YOU RECORD A TEAR? OR COUNT THEM AS THEY FALL? TO REMIND YOU OF WHAT?

EVERYTHING IN LIFE!"

"ONE DROP LEADS TO A STREAM! THE FLOW CAN NEVER OVERFLOW! AND WE WIPE IT AWAY AS IF IT NEVER EXISTED! WHO CAN TELL A TEAR TO STOP CRYING?

A HEART! A SOUL! CATCH IT!"

"A TEAR DOESN'T HAVE EYES, YET IT RETREATS! DON'T DOUBT GOD! HE EXISTS! GOD IS TRULY OUR SOURCE... OF LIFE!

'I AM ALPHA AND OMEGA' SIGNED GOD! THE BIBLE TOLD US SO!

I BELIEVE THE BIBLE! THE AMERICAN HISTORY BOOK!
'IN GOD WE TRUST! MAKE THOSE WORDS 'TRUE' AGAIN!'"

"I DIDN'T RUIN SUCCESS!
I SAVED IT!

GOD HAD TO COME
RESCUE AMERICA!

QUICK!

THE TEMPERATURE OF
HIS ANGER RISING!

FROM THE CLERGYMAN...
...TO THE SINNER! JUSTICE
WILL BE SERVED!

IT'S JUST A MATTER OF
TIME!

PRAY TO GOD FOR
PEACE!"

ADULT LIFE

"NAVIGATE LIFE!
TWISTS AND TURNS!"

"BE A LEADER... LEAD! LEAD GOOD QUALITY THINGS! WE HAVE BAD LEADERS EVERYWHERE! WHO WANTS TO SEE JUSTICE SERVED?"

PUNISHABLE

"I'M YOUR BEST PAIN! IT LEADS TO A CORRECTION OF LIFE IN LIFE!"

"YOU CAN TELL CREED
GREED!

MANY MAKE GREED
FAMILY! A BURDEN!

ENOUGH IS NEVER
ENOUGH!

NEVER MAKE GREED
FAMILY!

NEVER LET GREED BE
YOUR FRIEND!

DO NOT PET GREED OR IT
WILL BITE YOU!

IT IS A SIN!"

"MONEY IS A WEAPON...
TO FIGHT POVERTY!

WHAT ENDS UP
HAPPENING IS GREEDY
FOLKS, TAKE IT AWAY
FROM THE NEEDY FOLKS!

AND THE CYCLE NEVER
ENDS!

GOD IS A JUST GOD!
HE WILL REPAY!"

"IF I DON'T PUT MY PICTURE ON IT, IT WILL ANSWER MORE QUESTIONS!"

"A MAN NEEDS A WOMAN TO EXPLORE!

SEARCH THE GOLD MINES... ME!"

"MAN ENLISTS IN POVERTY WHEN HE MAKES LUST HIS HOME!"

"I WANT TO BEGAT **LOVE**... WHAT HAVE I DONE?"

“I WANT TO BE RICH IN **LOVE**, RICH IN **WISDOM**, RICH IN **INTIMACY**!”

A DIRTY SECRET

"MY BREASTS ARE
LOVELY FOR MY SPOUSE'S
EYES TO LOOK UPON, TO
CARESS, TO KISS, TO
COMFORT HIMSELF!
MY BREAST NEED HIM...
FAITHFUL IN POSITION TO
BE CARED FOR IN THE
LOVE MAKING PROCESS!
IT PRODUCES RESULTS!
EVERYTHING BETWEEN
MY LEGS BELONG TO HIM!
EVERY MOAN! HE
INDUCES! A RETURN ON
YOUR INVESTMENT IN
HOLY MATRIMONY!
A HEALTHY SEXUAL
SATISFYING MEMOIR TO
LOOK UPON! THAT

TANGIBLE TOUCH FROM A
HUSBAND'S POINT OF
VIEW!
LOVELY! LOVELY!
I WILL WAIT UNTIL MY
WEDDING DAY
FAITHFULLY! I'M NOT
FOOLING WITH
INFIDELITY THIS TIME
AROUND!
TRUST MY ORGASM!"

"A MAN'S DUTY!
A BED DUTY!
A SATISFYING DUTY!

ALL ELSE IS FALSE HOPE
OF FAILED COMMITMENT
AND WHOREDOM!

THERE IS NO STABILITY
IN THE FAME AND POISON
OF WHOREDOM!

LIFE LESSONS TAUGHT US
THAT!

GRIEVE LUST, BUT FOR A
MOMENT!

LOVE... TRUE LOVE
REIGNS!"

"I DEPENDED ON GOD TO FIND ME **TRUE LOVE**! AND HE SPOKE TO MY HEART!"

"GOD SPOKE TO MY HEART! I WAS INNOCENT IN MY PRAYERS FOR A MAN ONE DAY... THAT'S HOW MY LIFE, MY NEW LIFE STARTED! READ IT LIKE A CHAPTER BOOK!"

"THE ANTICIPATION OF PENETRATION IS EXCITING!

A MARRIAGE MADE IN HEAVEN!

THESE NOISES!

'HOW DO YOU WANT TO DO IT?'

ASK THESE QUESTIONS!"

"INTIMACY IS KEY!

A MUST!

MASTER IT!

BE THE MASTER KEY!

THE ENTRY TO EVERY
PART OF ME! ANY PART!

HOLY MATRIMONY!

KEEP IT!

PRIDE IS DANGEROUS!"

PUSSY

"THESE ARE THE GOOD
THINGS ABOUT PUSSY!
IT LOVES RELATIONSHIP!
HEALTHY RELATIONSHIP!
IT DOESN'T LIKE TO BE
ABUSED IN THE
FUNCTIONALITY OF IT!
IT INCREASES A
CONCENTRATION OF
THRUSTS! A DEGREE TO
THE STROKES OF MY
LOVER INSIDE OF ME!
IT IS NOT SIN, WHEN IT IS
MARRIED OFF ON A
WEDDING DAY!
PLAN IT! TO BE IN THE
GROOVE OF A MOTION
DETECTOR OF
LOVELINESS HUSBAND!

LJ HITE

ALL HUSBANDS ALIKE NAME THEIR PUSSY SOMETHING!"

"SQUISH AROUND INSIDE
IT! MEAT AND
TENDERIZER! WHICH IS
WHICH? THE MEAT OR
THE TENDER RISE HER?

HER LIPS! THE LIPS OF
THE VAGINA'S OPENING...
KISS THEM! THEY NEED
YOUR MOUTH FOR
INTRODUCING FOREPLAY!

PLAY FAIR! KEEP YOUR
LIPS GENTLY TEASING
THE TIP OF ECSTASY!

THIS LOVE IS GON' BE
RICH! MY MAN'S DICK IS
ALL I NEED!

ENVELOPE IT!

SWALLOW IT PUSSY!
ALL OF IT!

LET HIM GO DEEP...
DEEP... DEEPER!

I DARE NOT REST MY
SOUL UNTIL THIS LOVE
CLIMAX!"

"PUT YOUR FINGER,
GUIDE YOUR HANDS TO
FEEL MY SOFTNESS! THE
LIPS OF MY PUSSY DOES
NOT PURR, BUT IT WILL
MAKE ME HUM FOR YOU!

TOUCH IT! CAN YOU YOU
FEEL ITS MOISTURE?
EXPLORE EVERY AREA OF
MY GOLDEN CHAMBERS!

CLOSE YOUR EYES AND
MEMORIZE BY TOUCH
HOW IT FEELS BEFORE
YOU ENTER ME!

NOW LOOK AT ME!
EXAMINE EVERY PLACE
YOUR EYES DESIRE TO
SEE OF ME! I WANT YOU

TO KNOW THE PATH, A
PICTURE PERFECT VIEW
OF ME!

A PUSSY LOVER'S
ANTHEM!

PICTURE ME SINGING
YOUR NAME WHEN YOU
CAUSE ME TO RISE!

I LOVE YOU!"

"LET YOUR EYES
EXAMINE MY PUSSY
LIPS! PIGTAIL CURL THE
HAIRS OF MY PUSSY! OR
LET ME BE WAXED BALD!

WHEN MY PUSSY IS BALD
MY PUSSY LIPS LOOK BIG!
YUM YUM! WHEN MY
PUSSY BEARS HAIR, IT IS
AS A HAIRY
ESTABLISHMENT! MAY
MY HAIRS MEET YOUR
HAIRS!

ENTERTAINMENT FOR
THE PUSSY AND DICK!

DON'T COVER YOUR EYES,
COMFORT YOUR EYES!
FOR MY PUSSY IS YOURS...

RICH IN PUSSY SYRUP TO COVER THE THICKNESS OF YOUR APPETITE!"

"'NURSE ME' CRIES THE PUSSY!
HOW LONG WILL YOU TEASE MY PUSSY WITH YOUR HANDS, LIPS, MOUTH, OR THE TIP OF YOUR DICK?"

“ENTER ME SLOWLY SO I
CAN PREPARE FOR
TAKEOFF!

YOU ARE ABOUT TO TAKE
ME TO A LOT OF PLACES
ON YOUR DICK! A
SPOUSE’S MATE!

OH DICK, PLEASE ME!
DON’T DELAY WHAT YOU
WERE CREATED TO BE!

A STRONG MUSCLE THAT
MOVES A WOMAN’S
WHOLE BODY!”

"THE PENETRATION... LET IT BE SLOW TO THE RISING OF OUR CLIMATIC EXPERIENCE!

LET THIS MOMENT LAST AS LONG AS POSSIBLE, BEFORE OUR GREEDINESS OF ITS DESIRES MAKE US PEAK AN ORGASM!"

"LET ME TOUCH YOUR
DICK INSIDE OF ME! MAY
I PUT MY HAND AT THE
ENTRY POINT OF THESE
PUSSY LIPS AND FEEL
YOU INSIDE ME?

CAN I NOT ENJOY ALL OF
THIS MOMENT... FULLY?

THAT SHAFT THAT DIGS
INTO ME DEEP! GO DEEP
INSIDE MY PUSSY! THEN
PULL OUT, AND LET YOUR
DICK TIP AND KISS THE
EDGE OF MY
CLI-TOUR-US...
OK, CLITORIS!
MAY MY HAND GUIDE
YOUR DICK BACK INSIDE
ME!"

"SHOULD I HAVE STRETCHED BEFORE YOU PUT ME IN THIS POSITION?

I NEVER SIGNED UP FOR GYMNASTICS CLASS, AND YOU GOT ME TWISTED UP IN A MOOD POSITION!

MY LEGS!

HOLD MY LEGS! STAY THERE!

WE ARE BARELY GETTING STARTED!

UMMMMMMMMMMMMMM!"

"A MAN ASKED... WHAT IS GOLD?

A MARRIAGE MADE IN HEAVEN!

IT IS THAT DAY GOD CREATED EVE FOR ADAM!

TO BE FRUITFUL AND TO MULTIPLY!

MY 'GOLD' IS FRUIT!

EAT THERE OF IT WHEN THE RELATIONSHIP IS RIGHT!

IT IS THAT UN-LONELY PART OF MAN! THAT GOD CREATED IN THE GARDEN

OF EDEN!
IT IS VIRTUE!
THAT ENTRY WAY! TO
GOODNESS! INTIMACY IN
HOLY MATRIMONY!

VALUE GOLD... VALUE
SELF!

DON'T TAKE **LOVE** FOR
GRANTED!"

"DON'T GO TO SLEEP ON ME!"

"BEHAVIOR IS SO IMPORTANT IN REAL LIFE RELATIONSHIPS!

BE GOOD OR BE BAD!

YOU CAN'T BE BOTH!"

"I ASKED GOD FOR
SUCCESS IN LOVE!

I MADE QUITE OF MANY
MISTAKES THINKING
LUST WAS MY FRIEND!

LUST QUICKLY BECAME A
GRAVE... THE GRAVE!"

GOOD NEWS

"SUPERMAN HAD A HERO!

L O V E!

FOLLOW IT!

HE SHOWED COMMITMENT!

LOVE DOESN'T MAKE YOU LIE!

ESPECIALLY IF YOU'RE TRYING TO KEEP SOMEONE FOR A LONG TIME!"

"LET LOVE BE ALL YOU NEED!"

"THIS IS THE YEAR OF
HOPE!

THE YEAR OF
TWENTY TWENTY!

WE ARE IN A PANDEMIC
SEASON... STARVING FOR
LOVE!

HOPE RISES!
HOPE LIVES ON!
IN THE HEARTS OF
MANY!

THERE WAS A WAR ON
LOVE... GOD WON!

THE BLACK RACE AND
THE WHITE RACE WERE
DIVIDED...

BY WICKED PRESIDENCY
OF A WICKED LEADER'S
CARELESSNESS FOR
HUMANITY...
ALL OF HUMANITY!

A MAN CAN'T RUN A
COUNTRY... WITHOUT
PEOPLE!"

FAMINE

"WHAT WILL WE EAT?
SURELY, NOT LUST!
BECAUSE WE CANNOT
AFFORD IT!"

POVERTY

"POVERTY OF THE SOUL...
IS A LACK IN **LOVE**!"

"FAVOR FOUND SUCCESS
WANDERING!
AND LOOKING AROUND
FOR A HEART TO FAVOR
THE PURE IN HEART!
TO DO 'RIGHT' THINGS
BECAUSE IT IS THE RIGHT
THING TO DO!"

LJ HITE

"NOW ENJOY ME!"

ABOUT THE AUTHOR

"IF THEY ARE GOING TO TALK ABOUT YOU, LET THEM TELL A GOOD STORY... I WANT TO BE THE SUPERHERO, NOT THE ENEMY!"

Author's Remarks

"IT DOESN'T TAKE A MAN
ALL DAY TO FIND YOU!
HE CAN FIND PUSSY
ANYWHERE!

MEN USE EXCUSES LIKE
IT'S DIRTY MOP WATER!
THEY WANT THE DIRT,
INSTEAD OF
CLEANLINESS IN
STATURE!

THEY CREATE THEIR OWN
STATURE... AND SOME
MEN HAVE BECOME
MONSTERS!
FROM THE PULPIT, TO
THE DOOR!

THE BACK DOOR OF SECRETS, OF MANY SECRETS!"

NOTES:

NOTES:

NOTES:

NOTES:

NOTES:

NOTES:

NOTES:

NOTES:

www.ingramcontent.com/pod-product-compliance
Lightning Source LLC
Chambersburg PA
CBHW070633150426
42811CB00050B/281

* 9 7 8 0 9 7 6 5 8 9 8 5 3 *